Absolutely Typical

The Grouse Shooter

Absolutely Typical

words by Victoria Mather
pictures by
Sue Macartney-Snape

with a foreword by Auberon Waugh

THE BEST OF
SOCIAL STEREOTYPES
FROM THE
Telegraph Magazine

Methuen

First published in Great Britain in 1996
by Methuen London
an imprint of Reed International Books Ltd
Michelin House, 81 Fulham Road, London SW3 6RB
and Auckland, Melbourne, Singapore and Toronto

Reprinted 1996

ISBN 0 413 70200 6
A CIP catalogue record for this book
is available at the British Library

Designed by Christopher Holgate
Typeset by Dorchester Typesetting Group Ltd
Printed and bound in Great Britain
by Jarrold and Sons Ltd

Foreword

Many of our accepted social stereotypes go back before *Private Eye* to the misty, long lost days of P. G. Wodehouse, whose life covers the mighty span 1881–1975, and even before him to Oscar Wilde, who last drew breath on 30 November 1900. The startling thing is not so much that these stereotypes survive in our imaginations, but that they continue to flourish in contemporary society. Lady Bracknell may have become Lady Bagshot, now chiefly to be seen at family weddings; Lord Emsworth's dour gardener, Angus McAllister, may re-emerge here as the keeper (described, mysteriously, as the Jeeves of the outdoors) and the *Eye*'s Colonel Buffy Frobisher as Colonel Arbuthnot – the old colonel – who also, oddly enough, has a friend called Buffy. But they are all still with us, these great British comic archetypes, now given a new lease of life on the pages of the *Telegraph Magazine*.

There is an excellent reason why they should be gathered together in a book, but I will come to that later. A more immediate observation might be that whereas old stereotypes never seem to die – perhaps a Labour government will succeed in killing off the master of foxhounds when it passes laws to stop anyone hunting, but I suspect that the MFH will somehow survive abolition – there are new ones emerging the whole time.

Who would have guessed twenty years ago that the Australian nanny would play such a large part in our lives? Or that estate agents were the sort of people we would know socially, when the inadequate children of our friends were sucked into that notoriously crooked profession? Some of these stereotypes we may have observed and stored for ourselves, the best bring a sense of discovery. Many of us may have met the stage mother, Miriam, in a permanent state of indignation about the refusal of the theatrical profession to employ her extravagantly untalented daughter, Sammy-Jo, but most will not have identified her as a stereotype. In the same way, many will recognise the walker, but few will have distilled the essence of his appeal as Victoria Mather does.

It is a happy world, for the most part, which Victoria Mather describes and Sue Macartney-Snape illustrates. The picture of Marisa, the delicious young person from Notting Hill, and the father of her Scottish suitor, particularly sticks in the mind. Anger or scorn are seldom seen, though salient characteristics are keenly observed.

What is enticing about this book is its recognition of new and emerging stereotypes: 'In the eighties the wife-with-a-hobby was an interior decorator, nowadays she is a psychotherapist.' Not, please note, an aromatherapist. She is a seriously trained counsellor. One is reminded again and again of Marc, the late Mark Boxer, who made his particular study of the same social area. In addition to sheer entertainment value, the greatest use for this witty volume, with its perceptive illustrations, may be to help novelists and scriptwriters looking for secondary characters to fill out their plots. With a little shuffling of roles and sexes, you have in these forty-seven stereotypes a complete cast for about a hundred situation comedies.

Auberon Waugh
Combe Florey
February 1996

For Isabel Catto
and Winfreda Murray

No one likes to think of themselves as stereotypical but everyone is wonderfully happy to incriminate others: thank you for all the generous advice about the characters herein. And particular gratitude to Sarah Miller, who had the original idea, Emma Soames, for her enthusiasm to publish Social Stereotypes in the *Telegraph Magazine*, Mary O'Donovan, our editor at Methuen, who championed the book, and Richard Nourse, for his unflagging support.

V. M. and S. M.-S.

The Cad at Chelsea Flower Show

The spectre at the floral feast is the cad; he doesn't know a daisy from a delphinium but nevertheless runs a successful gardening business using a combination of Old Etonian swagger and transient jobbing Australians to service the gardens of non-gardeners from Chelsea to Clapham. He is the proselytiser of the terracotta pot, knowing that the pink geraniums (which he bought cheap at Covent Garden) will have to be replaced annually, an excuse to give Mrs Non-Gardener's little patio a good going over at fifteen pounds an hour. He'd certainly like to give the American beauty hovering in the Gothic garden a going over – what an exotic bloom, eh! Her manicure indicates that bedding out is not the sort of bedding she does. The cad's solitary prowl around the flower show is certainly more intent on picking up girls than gardening hints and to facilitate this end he wears a raffish leer and hair foaming over his collar like lobelia. The polo-neck jersey – a sign of dubious taste and intentions – is part of his uniform as the new milkman/gamekeeper of the moneyed classes: he services their herbaceous borders and hopes to continue his work for the good lady of the house indoors. The buttons on his blazer are of a club to which he has never belonged and his tartan trousers inspired by a menswear chain not a clan. The cad is social ground elder, a weed vigorously creeping over all those who think their gardens should be as tidy, chintzy and festooned as their drawing rooms.

The Waitress in Waiting

The waitress in London's fashionable restaurants is the Juno of the catering world. She descends from a Mount Olympus, where she is really studying thermodynamics or modelling, in order to favour customers with a bottle of Evian and the chicken and goat's cheese mousse. They had ordered the soup but are too overawed by the waitress's height (six foot), food-defying waistline (six inches) and sixth sense about their lack of importance to protest. She is waiting for clientele – Kenneth Branagh, perhaps, or Nigel Dempster – who can facilitate her progress from tables to tabloids via their stunned recognition of the insouciance required to declaim, 'Sorry, the risotto's off.' This week the waitress thinks she'll be a Sunday newspaper columnist – after all, Mariella Frostrup was – and the money must be terrific because she's served lots of journalists. 'Serve' is what she means when she condescends, accompanied by the chilly scarlet slash that is her smile, to respond to the frantic arm-waving of the famished. Sadly, the waitress does not realise that the tip is in proportion to her skirt length rather than her personality.

The Old Colonel

Colonel Arbuthnot spends many companionable hours pottering in the greenhouse with his gardener, Pluckrose, and chin-wagging about the old days. Pluckrose used to be his batman and now lives in the estate cottage of the Manor, Little Twining-in-the-Binding. The greenhouse is the Maginot Line between the colonel, Pluckrose and their respective wives. The colonel's other confidant is his chum Buffy. They are in perfect accord about the youth of today ('Don't know how lucky they are, what?'), politicians and the media ('All frightful second-raters'), Americans, women priests and the necessity of writing frequently to the newspapers about bringing back National Service. They meet for lunch at the Cavalry and Guards Club to reassure each other on these points and subscribe to the view that there was really only one war, it just had a lull in the middle to allow Jerry to regroup. Their idea of a cracking social occasion is the regimental dinner or Black Sunday, the Guards' memorial day when they march steadfastly through the rain with furled umbrellas and bowler hats. Colonel Arbuthnot's son does something in the City which he doesn't understand, but he loves having the grandchildren to stay and keeps sweeties in a jar by the Parker-Knoll where he and his excessively smelly water spaniel listen to *The Archers* each evening on the wireless.

The PR Girl

The PR girl has the personality of a Ladyshave: ostensibly smooth as silk but in fact a rapacious defoliant of the Right People at gallery openings, first nights, 'fragrance' launches, fashion shows and power breakfasts. Wherever two freeloaders and a glass of warm champagne are gathered together Patsy PR will be there, complete with haircut, clothes, jewellery and teeth all curiously angular and bright, and the glossy brochure of her latest client. Travel writers are cajoled with yurt and minaret camping holidays in Uzbekistan ('This year's most exciting new destination!'), restaurant critics threatened by the opening of a tapas bar in Notting Hill at which the gossip columnists are promised celebrities: 'I know Harold and Antonia are coming and Paula Yates is definitely invited!' Patsy always speaks in exclamation marks and her enthusiasm applies as much to a revolutionary stay-all-day lipstick ('You can kiss and it doesn't tell!') as to the publication of a Kurdish recipe book. She remembers everyone's name having once, during her early career in film PR, failed to recognise the critic Alexander Walker. The results were so emetic that she bought contact lenses and now addresses everyone personally whether she knows them or not – an alarming telephone technique. 'Is that Rebecca? Hi, how are you?' Rebecca Important isn't sure until she's discovered to whom she is speaking. 'Oh, this is Patsy of Catalyst PR and I was just wondering if you were coming to our launch of Fire-eater, the chilli-flavoured vodka, at the Groucho Club?' Living the dream of being Lynne Franks, Patsy is under the illusion that being unembarrassable makes her charming.

The Hairdresser

His dictatorial skills are legendary: the hairdresser is the Stalin of styling, the Pol Pot of the perm and he wields, along with his turbo-charged hairdryer, the power to make grown women cry. Addressing his client squarely in the mirror, he holds one limp, sad strand between two beringed fingers, grimacing, 'And who cut this last, madam?' To anyone already patronised by the shampooist's mantra, 'Are yer goin' out tonight then?' the implications are crushing. Lifestyle, as well as hair, is under examination in the salon intended to relieve victims of more money than is decent without a gun and a mask. Since the hairdresser became a celebrity he has ceased to be a confidante (semi-permanent psychotherapy); now he expects his clients to live up to him. He used to drop their names at bar-b-qs in Esher, now they fly him to their weddings in the West Indies. Women wait longer for him than for any other man, enthralled by his snip-happy powers to beautify or blight them with three months of Bad Hair Days while the layering grows out.

The Wedding Guest

Lady Bagshot regards fashion with Bracknellian hauteur. To buy a new dress for a wedding might be the sort of thing that goes on in Virginia Water but certainly not at Bagshot Magna. At the reception an ill-advised compliment on her hat, raffishly trimmed by the gamekeeper's wife (who does millinery with the WI), elicits a snort of disgust. Lady Bagshot does not believe in personal remarks, although she interrogated her god-daughter Mary severely when informed she was to marry a banker. The explanation that a merchant banker is not quite the same as the little man who sits thumbing greasy notes behind the grille in Barclay's has failed to entirely satisfy her. In her day one didn't have a banker to luncheon, let alone marry one. Still, he seems a decent fellow and the engagement ring is a very good piece. Lady Bagshot has an eagle eye for jewellery, possessing a formidable amount of it, and the Bagshot pearls do much to enhance an *embonpoint* that looks like a floral ski slope. Her large plastic watch contrasts oddly with her diamonds but is essential for myopically monitoring every moment spent away from the herbaceous border. Fond as she is of her god-daughter, the lupins need attention. Having stumped round the marquee twice, she considers escape before the speeches. Too late. She is cornered by the bridegroom's mother who has heard so much about her from dear Mary. Lady Bagshot concludes from the carapace of make-up in front of her that dear Mary should confine her mother-in-law to every other Christmas. Finally on her way, Lady Bagshot catches sight of herself in the hall mirror. It is rather a splendid hat, isn't it?

The Tourists

Back home in Kellogg, Iowa, Elmer and Belle-Mae had thought a 'hotel in the bustling heart of London' sounded just the place to start their tour of 'Yurrup'. Unfortunately, they did not know how bustling the Cromwell Road would be. The hotel's proximity to Harrods is notional, particularly to one whose poor feet are as much of a trial to her as Belle-Mae's, and the concierge seems incapable of either speaking English or getting tickets to *The Phantom of the Opera*. All in all, Britain is a disappointment, with the exception of Scotland ('Which isn't in England, Belle-Mae'), seen on their ScotOption weekend break. After Mel Gibson's *Braveheart*, Belle-Mae was determined to 'do' the Highlands and the kilted courier took their photograph in Glencoe, which even Elmer admits is awesome. Otherwise, he thinks it is a doggone shame that Windsor Castle was built so close to the airport, fails to understand why the Brits drive on the wrong side of the road and rates the sluggish demeanour of the Thames far inferior to the crystalline waters of the North Skunk river back home. After queuing in the rain for two hours, Belle-Mae was mighty upset that the Queen had unaccountably nipped out during their tour of Buckingham Palace. Her shell suit and his shorts barely have time to dry out between trips to Madame Tussaud's and the Tower of London – it was never like this on their last holiday in Florida. The galleries full of old art may be wonderful (and at least dry) but London's litter, beggars, incomprehensible public transport system and exorbitant taxi fares ('Pound for dollar on that meter, Belle-Mae') confirm his suspicions that this degenerate country would never have won the war without wholesome American intervention.

The Earth Mother

Cressida is largely unconcerned by the neuroses that beset other mothers: dogs licking the spoons in the open dishwasher and toys on the staircase that could act as skateboards to a broken leg for Daddy. Other mothers are really lawyers, accountants or columnists for Sunday newspapers with children on the side, but Cressida is mother to all, including her husband, Adrian. He is a composer whose music resembles whale song. Divine with his children, he is hopelessly impractical. Cressida serenely changes all plugs and fuses, tends the organic vegetable plot and unblocks the main drain while cooking casseroles on the wood-burning stove. She comes from a large family and is impervious to noise and mess; her bedroom is a swirl of Habitat bedlinen and floating garments from Antiquarius. She shares her husband's shirts and jerseys and, since her remarkable bosom is a stranger to the bra, it doesn't matter that they slither off her ample, unstrapped shoulders. She still has the courage to swathe her hips in leggings. Cressida cuts the children's hair with kitchen scissors which are later, if not simultaneously, used to cut home-cured bacon for a gritty spinach salad. This is grown in profusion between the kitchen and the donkey field so it doesn't matter whether there are five or fifteen around her scrubbed pine table, whose centre-piece consists of forget-me-nots and limp cow parsley collected by the children and arranged in jam jars. Adrian, an only child, is in bliss with all this careless security. Each night he goes to sleep pillowed by Cressida's largesse.

The Wimbledon Fan

Wimbledon is the emotional high point of the year for Aileen, a sports director at a very good comprehensive in Birmingham. She applies for her tickets in the public ballot by December 31st and obtains two for the first week. To the uninitiated, like Gwen who teaches geography, this implies a couple of wet afternoons watching British players being thrashed by volatile Romanians, but Aileen knows of the wealth of good matches on the outside courts. 'Frankly, Gwen, you stand more chance of seeing your hero Agassi – a shameless exhibitionist, I should tell you – during the first week than you ever will later. Last year he was so close to me, I could have touched him.' Gwen and the rest of the staff room are tremendously appreciative of this brush with greatness. Aileen will then let slip that she also has tickets for the second week obtained through her local tennis club, to which she has belonged for twenty years. Armed with a cool-bag of sandwiches and bitter lemon (the prices for refreshments at Wimbledon being wicked), she punctuates matches with time spent at the railing outside the players' dressing rooms, hoping to see Fernandez or Sabatini. Aileen thinks women's tennis is shamefully underrated – nothing will be quite the same now that Martina has retired, a blow equalled only by the departure of Dan Maskell to the celestial commentary box. Aileen reveres tradition; the legends of Bill Tilden and Little Mo are as vivid to her as the performance of any bouncing, bronzed babe battery-farmed in the Florida tennis centres. That they should be so lucky with personal trainers, sponsored track suits and Sledgehammer racquets – if only, mourns Aileen, her own career having peaked in dim gold letters on her club's doubles' shield.

The Network Marketeer

Ever since Sally began selling Glamrocks costume jewellery she has met so many wonderful friends and become so *motivated*. Her husband is staggering under negative equity and Lloyd's losses, the children have gone to university and Sally has been reborn as a proselytiser of the Glamrocks Zodiac Collection: 'We give you the moon and the stars to wear.' Of course it isn't really 'selling' (Sally doesn't think selling sounds very nice); there is a proper business structure – Sally has been to 'orientation seminars' – and everyone is doing it now. No dinner party off the Fulham Palace Road would be complete without the ritual unfurling of the Glamrocks suedette jewellery roll, and Sally has discovered a brave new world of water filters, juice extractors and vacuum cleaners being purveyed by minor aristocracy and MPs' wives. 'Needs must. We're all business people now,' says Sally crisply, piling on the pearls to enhance an outfit that looks like an explosion in a ribbon factory. She never thought she'd get involved when her friend Tricia sold her the enamel frog earrings, but then people kept asking (in Harrods even – can you imagine?) where she got her amusing jewellery. So Tricia recruited her and she's recruited Janie and Carolyn and lots of Wandsworth wives. Now she has her little empire and although her husband said it all sounded like a glorified Tupperware party, he didn't complain when Sally paid for their holiday in Provence. These are the sort of rewards you earn with a marvellous product, for which Sally's fervent belief gleams madly from beneath her blue Margaret Thatcher eyeshadow. She's off soon on an incentive training weekend in Cannes. This isn't like a proper job, you know. It's fun. You should join, you really should.

The Trendy Vicar

The retirement of dear old Canon Wheezel strikes dread into Aga saga land: the rural idyll of carols, harvest festival and evensong will be shattered by the arrival of a trendy vicar. The Rev. Trevor constitutes even more of an insult than a woman priest. As soon as the verger sees Trevor's beard, he spreads hideous visions of guitar music, total immersions and the *Good News Bible* throughout the village. He is right about the *Good News Bible*. Trevor means well; he is always smiling earnestly and asks old Lady Armitage, 'Does the Bible speak to you?' She is too overcome by the bumper sticker on Trev's Astra – 'Carpenter seeks Joiners' – to respond with civility. The fellow doesn't play bridge and his wife, Lucy, is a vegan. Trevor would be so much more suited to a suburban parish with opportunities for victim support groups and a church where overhead projectors might illustrate his sermons. Such innovations are unpopular at St Mary the Virgin, Ridingwold. Still, the Renault Espace families adore his Sunday school and the rap nativity play. His lay readers are young professionals in jerseys who share Trevor's concern about poverty, about which they know little beyond the church collection for Shelter at Whitsun. At Lucy's pasta and bean salads, Trevor talks vividly about 'being a Christian'. His face, usually a pale imitation of the Turin Shroud, glows with fervour in lieu of alcohol as he shares his thoughts of St Paul and Tony Blair. Lady Armitage could not dine with a man wearing such dreadful shoes.

The Mistress

Easter is a dreary festival for the mistress. Her lover is spending quality time with his family and she is alone with the Tibetan spaniel. Unlike Christmas, when even a forty-year-old may be forgiven for going home to mother, the Easter holiday is one which ostensibly unattached women usually enjoy with friends. But the friends have children and as a mistress she dislikes children because she does not have any. The ticking of her biological clock during the Easter egg hunt is a noisome reminder of the real truth: that all the passion spent on sex in the afternoon cannot compensate for the school run in the morning. Waiting for *his* call from a pay phone near the pub, the mistress's emotions seethe in a swirl of Sancerre. A nice convent girl with a career in merchant banking should not have come to this. When he hasn't rung by Saturday she could cheerfully boil the Easter bunny. There's nothing on the television, one (and one's mobile telephone) can only spend so much time at the gym, the hairdresser is shut and the manicurist has gone to Spain. Anyway, those who grapple with Powerbooks rather than pruning, ponies and petit point rarely chip their nails. The mistress's gay confidant, Clive, says that one of the world's greatest lies is, 'I never sleep with my wife.' *He* rings on Sunday. 'But darling, I just couldn't phone before, we've been in church.' The mistress replies tartly that she is going to tell all to the parish magazine. On Monday she knows that It's Over; he is never going to leave his wife. On Tuesday he turns up with a bottle of champagne and they fall into bed.

The Keeper

The keeper is the Jeeves of the outdoors. A man may divorce his wife, despise his children and dismiss the cook but he will never, ever fall out with dear old Alec. This Titan in tweed is venerated by men and dogs and he is firm but fair with both; under-keepers, ghillies, beaters, spaniels and labradors are the foot soldiers in his private army. The lore of the woods and moors is in his bones, giving him dominion over all he surveys while he leans on his stout knobkerrie enjoying a quiet smoke. A dour pessimist, he discourages any expectation of sport with a litany of disease, vermin, drought (but excessive rain during nesting), ramblers, poachers and the anti-blood sports townie bastards. He has a healthy suspicion – veiled by bushy-eyebrowed grandeur – of the Huns, Yanks and callow merchant bankers who shoot on let days, however generous their tips. The keeper knows the difference between a gentleman's sincere appreciation and the new-minted attempt of Johnny Foreigner to curry his favour. That difference lured his son away from the estate into computer electronics.

The Family on Holiday

The holiday is doomed from the moment the Cherokee jeep is grid-locked by roadworks at Chiswick. Charles tells Caroline that they should have left Fulham earlier, everyone knows it's a nightmare getting to Heathrow. Caroline, knuckles white on the steering wheel, asks why he didn't leave the office on time. The teenagers, Emily and Edmund, say they never wanted to go to Tuscany anyway, all their friends are going to Rock. Caroline, slamming through the gears, shouts that the weather in Cornwall is hideous and she doesn't want *her* children getting drunk in the Mariners and bonking on the beach. Arthur, the family afterthought, grizzles that he'd have liked to go to EuroDisney. Caroline bursts into tears. The villa sounded so ideal in the classified columns of the *Spectator*: 'Enchantingly remote farmhouse near Cortona; maid, tennis court, pool. No telephone, so utter peace.' 'Remote' turns out to mean two kilometres up a track unnegotiable by hire car. The maid doesn't speak English, it is too hot to play tennis and Arthur falls into the pool within twenty minutes of arrival. Charles, hitherto so pleased with his mobile telephone, finds it only works from the far corner of the olive grove. He looks ludicrous in the Marks & Spencer leisurewear bought by his wife. Arthur's eczema is furiously exacer-bated by the heat and Emily's best friend, who comes to stay in the second week, cannot eat wheat ('Mummy said to be sure and tell you it gives me coeliac disease, Aunt Caroline'), so no one can have pasta. When Caroline gets free for one afternoon in Florence – where she went to finishing school in 1970 – she discovers it has become park-and-ride. On the second-last day Edmund falls in love with doe-eyed Dolcelatta from the village trattoria: 'Oh Mum, do we *have* to go home?'

The Scottish House Party

Marisa's one concession to travelling north of the border is her tartan skirt. Well, they wear tartan up there, don't they? That her minimalist interpretation of this fact bears no relation to the plaid horse blanket worn by her hostess is a matter of sublime indifference to Marisa. Nor does she understand that by wallowing in an enormous bath while reading *Birdsong*, she deprives the rest of the house of hot water. 'Hasn't Jamie explained to her about the three-inch-bath rule?' hisses Lady McSporran, appalled that her son has brought someone to stay who wears black on the moor. Sir Hamish McSporran of that Ilk, hovering paternally next to her, considers Marisa a charming child. But, since Patrick Cox loafers haven't yet penetrated Perthshire, he regrets that those funny shoes fail to do her legs justice. He takes considerable trouble to teach her the house rules of racing demon. Marisa, who had hazy expectations of life beyond Notting Hill Gate, thinks Scotland is totally cool. She loves lying in the heather picnicking, and sitting by the river in the evening watching Jamie fishing, smoking madly to keep the midges at bay. Her idea of entertainment has hitherto been a Tarantino movie at the Gate cinema, but she loves the arcane after-dinner games over which Sir Hamish presides with his wee dram. She loves being twirled through Scottish dancing by all the men. She loves Jamie, a passion consolidated by seeing him in a kilt. And, since she is in love, Marisa fails to notice either the filthiness of the food or, when she waves away the grouse at dinner, Lady McSporran's dire suspicions of vegetarianism. Secure in the sunlit idyll, Marisa dreams of chucking her waitressing job at 192 and living at Sporran Castle with Jamie forever. She has never seen it in the mist, rain and toe-curling cold when the fire smokes.

The Cabbie

The morose, nicotine-stained, *Sun*-streaked philosophical edge of the taxi-driver has been blunted since the departure of Lady Thatcher from the world stage. Love her or hate her, she was a proper leader, if you ask me. John Major, he couldn't lead anybody up the garden path, now where did you say you were going, love? St James's? Oh dear, oh dear, not in a hurry, I hope, it'll be murder getting round Buckingham Palace with that new road layout. Maggie would never have allowed it, I mean is this a capital city or a theme park for Japanese tourists? In all the years I've been driving this cab I've never seen anyone get hit outside Buck House, those Nips ought to remember who won the war. My old dad was in Burma, wonders what he fought for now that mugging old ladies is a ticket to a safari holiday. Everyone just thinks they can do nothing and earn a lot of money, if you ask me. That Barings lot were just greedy, if you ask me. Look at the Queen, it was rack and thumbscrews before she paid income tax like the rest of us and you'd think she'd do something about these traffic lights in front of her own house. But, if you ask me, she can't even manage her own family. Charlie'll marry that Camilla Park n' Ride because the bishops are all poofs. Ooooh, have you got anything smaller? Thanks, love, here's a blank receipt. I once had that Ned Sherrindan Morley in the back of my cab.

The Edinburgh Festival Comedian

Being funny is a feminist issue. Men are a joke, aren't they? It's a complete joke that only one woman has ever won the Perrier Award – it's just jokes for blokes. In fact, jokes are a joke, being phallocentric and patriarchal. Femina Dickeridge (not the name by which she was known at Cheltenham Ladies' College) is currently working up a really aggressive joke about Hugh Grant for her midnight act at the Gilded Balloon. By day she strides the Royal Mile distributing leaflets advertising *Femina In Yer Face*, reassuring students and bemused American tourists that it is the radical alternative to alternative comedy. The orange hair, black roots, red lipstick and Dusty Springfield eye make-up spell out 'anger'. Femina is angry that she was born Charlotte in Godalming. She sloughed off the accent at a provincial university and piled on the fat in protest at the male perception of beauty. Down south she has a perfectly nice husband, but for the purposes of her act she affects to be a lesbian, her only concession to fashion. In the bright, white light of her 'venue' (theatres are middle class) she berates the audience with a routine about men having babies, with expletives that would make Bernard Manning blush and, as a finale, why only a man could have invented the Femidom. Afterwards she drinks lager from the bottle and accepts a cigarette, despite doubts about the morality of smoking because tobacco manufacturers are manipulative capitalists. The return to a mouldy basement is not the stuff of stardom but then anyone who opts for comfort at the Balmoral Hotel has sold out, haven't they? Strange that, once asleep, Femina dreams of an offer from Channel 4.

The Bookie

Win or lose, it has always been a terrible day for the racecourse bookie. Quite apart from the rain and the favourite winning the 3.30, things aren't what they used to be, he can tell you. It's the Lottery, that's what it is. Given the choice between Anthea Turner and a nice day out at Haydock Park the punters have gone doolally. Not that there are many big punters around nowadays, not like it was in his father's day; but there wasn't racing on the telly then, was there? The bookie, like the British farmer, is a fund of pessimism. Fortified by a tub of Barrie Cope's jellied eels and three fingers of Scotch ('Mind what you're doing with that water, lad'), he stands rock-solid over the battered Gladstone bag which brims with the punters' tenners and has his name painted on the side. Should he have to delve into his coat – made spherical by having more pockets than a poacher's – to extract a roll of reserve funds, he'll be a truly unhappy man. His clerk, a miniscule human calculator of the odds, will know better than to ask for a lift home in the Jag. The Sunday round of golf, while the wife is making the roast, will be tinged with a sadness exacerbated by the '*You* must have had a good day, Joe' jibes of his compadres at the bar who lost their shirts. Back home in the half-timbered, pebble-dash villa, Joe will lugubriously plan the family's Christmas holiday in a five-star hotel in Marbella before walking his very small, white and fluffy shih-tzu called Desert Orchid – or Awkward to those less prejudiced than the bookie.

The Dog Walker

One's dog walker is more important than one's nanny. Any fool can look after the children but darling little Muffet needs the undivided attention of Dorothy, a Viyella Valkyrie in sensible shoes, whose stentorian tones can stop a labrador at twenty paces in Kensington Gardens. Even Muffet, an intellectually challenged spaniel, behaves herself with Dorothy who perfectly understands (unlike Muffet's mistress) that a dog needs routine, discipline and plenty of good fresh air. When Dorothy arrives promptly at eleven a.m. Muffet does a little dance in the white W11 portico before joining an Afghan, various wirey Battersea mutts, a Norwich terrier and the highly strung setter already shaking Dorothy's ancient Volvo with vociferous excitement. The smell inside is an awesome combination of engrained dog hair, setter slobber and Mr Woo, a Pekingese with breath like an acetylene torch. But Dorothy is not squeamish about such things and fearlessly confronts Mr Woo's doting owner with his dental deficiencies: 'He really ought to eat more biccie, Lady Trimble, but once he's moulted his tail will bloom like a rare orchid.' Lady Trimble is tickled pink. During those weekends to which dogs are disinvited (Muffet once dug through a sofa in order to retrieve a ball), Dorothy has her regulars to stay in her garden flat. The solid, red-brick Victorian block is where she has lived ever since her marriage to an army colonel. The marriage did not work out but Dorothy remained, along with some very lumpy furniture much improved by having dogs on it. They are her companions now and their social life in the park is more intense than that of any child. On a Saturday night Dorothy is quite content with a stout whisky, *Casualty* and Muffet's invaluable help doing the crossword.

The Prep School Master

Mr Carstairs has always looked middle-aged and dishevelled, like an academic Lord Emsworth. When he was a youth, one sock was perpetually at half-mast, his jumper ornamented with gravy stains and his pocket money eluded him through a hole in the lining of his tweed jacket. Long trousers now conceal the sock problem but the jumper and jacket insignia have remained consistent; those pesky new pound coins just will work their way through the seams. The boys can run rings round their prep school master (whom they call the Fossil behind his back) and only much, much later, when doing the crossword on the way to the City, may they appreciate the easy familiarity he established between them and Eng. Lit. His real love of Shakespeare and the romantic poets transcends the paper dart tendency and is occasionally rewarded by a child who actually understands what he's going on about. Of course, Mr Carstairs wanted a fellowship at Oxford rather than taking detention on a wet bank holiday Monday because the headmaster's gone to Paris on Eurostar. Yet he has borne his rejection by the groves of academe without bitterness, enduring generations of little perishers by deceiving himself that he's Captain Grimes. At home, he deducts marks for spelling from young Blenkinsop's essay on 'Ode to a Nightingale', opens a bottle of claret for dinner and watches *Inspector Morse*. After Sports Day – hideous scenes between competitive fathers – he and Mrs Carstairs are going to tootle round France in the motor. Call him old-fashioned, call him a fossil but none of his pupils will ever confuse *The Tempest* with a pop group.

The Fashion Editor

The fashion editor is perpetually beset by anxieties. Will she be in the front row at the Paris collections? Have the designers filled her hotel suite with presents? Is the suite bigger, and in a better hotel, than that of her rival from *Gloss* magazine? Why isn't she married? Where in this crazy Prada bag is her chewing gum? In a petulant demonstration of power she sends back some of the presents, asking for them in a different colour. Life on the cutting edge of a gilt chair means that each spring and autumn the fashion editor witnesses a parade of eternal youth which reinforces her insecurities. Her magazine will surely soon replace her with one of the elfin, black-clad slips of girls who actually understand the new Zen-spaghetti designs of Sushi Zucchini. In a maudlin haze of cigarettes and white wine she contemplates life without samples, discounts or a husband. At the time when her contemporaries were dating, the fashion editor was always on swimsuit shoots in St Lucia. Now, if anyone asks, she says there simply isn't room for a man in her life because her cupboards are all full. Little of their contents has accompanied her to Paris since she borrows the latest designs, emerging from the long winter of taupe and bitter chocolate in pastels. Now she is set to find six approximately similar garments in order to describe the New Look ('Spangled tweed is sparkling through'). That white stilettoes are coming back this summer is more world-shattering to the fashion editor than Bosnia; that she will wear them herself is why, in choosing to be trendy rather than a *grande dame*, she ends up as comic and absurd.

The Private Doctor

Dr Marwood, neat and polished as a billiard ball, is an oasis of reassurance in the midst of the Hon. Natasha Fretful's appalling illness. In the maw of the National Health Service she would merely be judged to have a cold but here, across the soothing yardage of the doctor's reproduction mahogany partner's desk, she can be confident of a virus. Or, at the very least, of a 'Dear me, Natasha, you have quite clearly been overdoing it at Sotheby's. Working you hard on the front desk, are they?' as his Mont Blanc pen travels across a white pad, prescribing something she could easily buy over the counter at Boots. 'You could buy this over the counter at Boots,' he says thoughtfully, for Natasha looks woefully inadequate for the decision between Nightnurse and Lemsip. It is then that she bursts into tears, an eventuality fielded by the discreet box of man-sized tissues. Between noisome blows and gulps, Natasha confides that It Is All Over: Rupert has dumped her, her life has ended, she cannot sleep. Dr Marwood puts the tips of his fingers thoughtfully together and proposes a B12 injection; seeing him glide across to the mini-bar of drugs and potions, Natasha is comforted by his pinstriped suit and Oxford brogues (although when Daddy had his heart thingy in the middle of the night, Dr Marwood turned up in an improbable leather bomber jacket and on a motor bike). Ushering her out of the pale yellow consulting room, Dr Marwood smiles a 'Just one moment' to patients engrossed, according to age, in back copies of *Country Life* or the toy-box, and seeks his secretary's help in extracting their records from the new CD-Rom system. He muses that he will receive an invitation to Natasha and Rupert's wedding within the year.

The Cleaning Lady

Sophie Young-Married tidies the house before the cleaning lady arrives. Mrs Green, who calls her Sophie although Sophie calls her Mrs Green, used to work for the previous occupants of the Old Manor, a stentorian dowager and four labradors, and sees no reason why anything should change. Sophie thinks she's like Mrs Danvers with Pledge, but help has been impossible to find in the village since everyone went to work in the hypermarket. So she makes Mrs Green cups of tea ('Typhoo please, dear, not that nasty Earl Grey'), listens to the saga of her bunions and is suitably grateful to have the dust rearranged in her drawing room. Mrs Green implies by heavy wheezing that every photograph frame and bibelot is a personal affront and she made such pointed remarks about drip-dry and easy-care that Sophie gave up insulting her with the ironing and now sends the sheets to the laundry. As a gesture of approval, Mrs Green gave her a very woolly marrow personally grown by Mr Green. Thanking her profusely, Sophies thinks longingly of Spanish Maria and the simple life left in London.

The Famous Author

The famous author is a work of fiction equal only to his own best-selling novels. The buttons on his blazer imply a regimental bearing, the signet ring a family crest. Glossy, with tremendously clean fingernails, hair shining with Trumper's unguents and highlights invisible to the naked eye, the author's natural habitat is the provincial book signings at which he looks suave drinking Soave. He is inordinately proud of the blue, penetrating gaze (contact lenses) with which he transfixes housewives called Jenny – 'Is that with a "y" or an "ie"?' he twinkles raffishly, pen poised, as they part with the requisite twenty pounds. He oozes through radio programmes like an oil slick, relishing in retelling anecdotes about himself and leaves *Loose Ends* under the impression that he has been funnier than Ned Sherrin. He is rather short, a reason why he is so ambitious; the stripes of his Turnbull & Asser shirt are rather broad, his laugh rather loud and his overweaning desire to join the Garrick rather wide of the mark.

The Therapist

In the eighties the wife-with-a-hobby was an interior decorator, nowadays she is a psychotherapist. Rupert and Katie are long gone to university so the au pair's pit on the half-landing of the large, empty house has been redecorated (the therapist kept her trade accounts) as a consulting room. It has soothing Venetian green walls and minimalist goblet pleating on the linen curtains, pelmets and chintz being regrettably at odds with Prozac and angst. The wing chairs look professional yet relaxed, the therapist thinks tentatively, four years of psychoanalytical training having refined her designer instincts. The depressed, bereaved, childless, boyfriendless, divorced and stressed-out-by-having-had-to-find-Hampstead who slump opposite her are treated with a kindly but detached concern that owes more to her old nanny than to the etiquette of the therapeutic relationship. A clock strategically placed behind the patient enables her to say briskly, 'You must understand that you're in self-denial, but that's all for this afternoon,' at precisely ten to the hour. Her husband, a florid investment banker, thinks damned counselling is a lot of caring nineties' rot but is relieved that the furtive consumption of his vodka has diminished. The liability at dinner parties is that he'll overhear his wife banging on about Jung and the mysticotranscendent approach to correct the chairman of Lazard Warburg's impression that she is an aromatherapist.

The Cosmetics Salesgirl

Charlene is in the front line of every department store's olfactory offensive. Since the perfumery hall is *en route* to all departments, customers need a gas mask to reach haberdashery, so enthusiastic is the cosmetics salesgirl. Armed with a Flit gun of Milliondollars, the new scent by Manfredo Extravaganza, she intones, 'Good morning, madam, would you like to try Milliondollars? It's a fresh bouquet of jasmine, musk and tea rose . . . No? Well, have a nice day.' Charlene, with her improbable hairdo, her toothsome smile made gigantic by Prune Sizzle lip liner, returns to the Extravaganza stand. It is laden with jazzy unguents for the ageing undead over thirty. Charlene, her own visage cemented with Extravaganza's Silken Porcelain foundation, doesn't want to believe in old age, though she can see it happening in the sad, untended faces of her clients. 'You've a lovely complexion, madam,' she says brightly. 'Why don't you try our Satinette moisturiser for delicate skins?' Her training course at the polytechnic (now a university) inculcated Charlene with the benefits of a positive approach and a touching belief in her product. 'The Satinette range is suffused with natural herbs, the cowslip face mask is luvverly. Then there's our Parma Violet anti-wrinkle cream. Isn't the mauve packaging attractive? This Silken Sorrel lipstick would suit you, madam,' she adds kindly, batting eyelashes tarmacked with Silken Midnight mascara. In order to escape from Charlene's manicured toils, madam spends £150 on lettuce eye gel. Home in Romford after another day at the rock face of beauty, Charlene fantasises that she is Elizabeth Hurley.

The Hypochondriac

He never has a cold, he has 'flu' which rapidly transmutes into a virus, which will probably become double pneumonia and most certainly, at the very least, have gone down on to his chest by the morning. He piteously asks his beloved whether she thinks it would be all right if he took two more Nurofen. Beloved, toiling up and down the stairs with tempting trays of consommé, mutters that cyanide might be more effective. But martyr as the hypochondriac may be to passing germs, he is impervious to irony. Were he self-analytical as well as self-diagnostic, he would recall that many good women and true have left following the nostalgic anecdote about his old mum soothing his fevered brow with 4711 cologne. Indigestion bodes an incipient heart attack. A sore throat is obviously the beginning of 'the bug that has been going round the office'. He shakes the thermometer in disbelief as the mercury remains stubbornly below the little red line. Will a Fisherman's Friend interfere with the antibiotics he's sure to have to take? He braces himself for the worst by gathering a repellent prep school dressing gown around his tortured body. Every muscle aches, his back (always dodgy, he can't lift a thing) is a real killer and his secretary kindly reassures him that Tracy in accounts was sick all night when she had 'the raging Beijing'. He's sure he heard on the car radio that it is the worst epidemic since the flu in 1957. This is almost too exciting for someone whose idea of a dangerous drug is hot lemon and honey. The hypochondriac's one regret in life is that he has never really been ill.

The Stage Mother

Miriam is outraged; yet another casting of urchins for *Oliver!* has inexplicably been and gone without her adorable Sammy-Jo having won a part. Her freckles, her carrot-coloured curls, not to mention her piping rendition of 'Consider Yourself at Home' are so cute that she must have been auditioned by blind men. Miriam will have to call Cameron Mackintosh herself. He wants cheeky? Sammy-Jo can do cheeky at the toss of her pony-tail. He wants cherubic? Sammy-Jo, christened Samantha Joanne, has the disposition of the Angel Gabriel. That her daughter is extravagantly untalented is not a thought which has ever clouded Miriam's mental horizon. The child has indubitably inherited the maternal genius nipped in the bud when Miriam married a handsome night-club accompanist. This individual now spends rather more time down the pub accompanying a pint of beer, and Miriam has invested all her hopes of fame and fortune in Sammy-Jo's nascent career at the Italia Conti school. 'The child came out of the womb tap-dancing,' she says, her frontage, which is arranged like rockets going off in opposite directions, heaving with pride as she watches the frantic little legs and the hands revolving like windmills. Failing *Oliver!*, or a revival of *Annie,* there is always pantomime and Miriam peruses the *Stage* for any news of tap-dancing mice required for Cinderella's transformation scene in Solihull. Yet, in the spare seconds between Sammy-Jo's extra voice-training, gymnastics and ice-skating classes (well, they are doing *Aladdin* on ice this year) her day-dream is of a television commercial. Just look how far Patsy Kensit has come since she endorsed peas.

The Clubbable Man

He's a wit, he's a wag, he is the ornament on life's cream damask sofa. The clubbable man is abroad not only in the Garrick but also in the most amusing drawing rooms, when not writing elegantly on such as 'Istanbul – The Byzantine Jewel' for an in-flight magazine in return for air tickets. His mother was a gravel-voiced icon who might have put Edith Evans in the shade had she not married a peer and been subsumed by a passion for herbaceous borders and Pekingese. His father knew everyone, was a member of everything and cared not a jot for anyone – other than his wife and, strangely, the Pekingese – which is why the son has an inexhaustible collection of anecdotes about the great, the good and Sir John Gielgud. Flirtatious, bibulous, ineffably charming and entirely at ease with his own success as a biographer and Grecophile, the clubbable man is a serial husband. His first wife was an artist, his second a novelist and his third a psychiatrist. They are all rather beautiful, in a Hampstead sort of way, but friends long for the weeks when the present incumbent is plying her trade in New York so that they can have the clubbable man's bonhomie all to themselves. The point of him is that he disseminates his enthusiasm for their new house, his new travel book, his forthcoming lecture cruise, upgrades on British Airways, Delphi, Aphrodisias and the latest theatrical scandal with equal vigour. He always knows someone you know, and assumes you know them equally well, which is cosy and the reason why he is everyone's best friend after several minutes. He treats gossip as wonderfully important and imparts it without malice, and so, by the end of the evening, he has been asked to stay in every villa, chalet and house party available in the room.

The Opera Lover

Nothing annoys the opera lover more than some frightful little man from Hai-Ho Inc. cluttering up her husband's seats in the Royal Opera House. Her husband is a merchant banker and the seats are actually his company's, but Aurelia regards them *extremely* proprietorially. 'James, what on earth is the point of taking Japanese clients to Covent Garden? Surely they don't understand anything except *Madame Butterfly,* and anyway I've invited the Studley-Montmorencys.' Sophia Studley-Montmorency and Aurelia used to share a flat in South Ken in the far-off days when they were working – Aurelia had a nice little job in a Cork Street gallery – and often hopped on the Piccadilly line to go and see Puccini from the gods.

Having re-read the plot, with scoring, in Kobbé's *Complete Opera Book* while at the hairdresser, Aurelia arrives early at the Royal Opera House. James has arranged the champagne with Alex the barman and the usual table tucked to the right of the orchestra stalls, so much more discreet than the Crush Bar despite the proximity to the ladies' loo. During the first interval they have Chablis and smoked salmon (Aurelia dashes to remove the cling wrap from the plates as soon as the curtain falls); during the second, Burgundy and roast beef salad. Albert Roux it isn't, but such a splendid way of shedding clients by 10.30 p.m.; friends they take to the Savoy for pudding and a drink. Aurelia says that the new American soprano has much more purity than Mirella Freni in the 1986 production. She did not actually see this but has the CD in her car. Sophia's husband counteracts with cheery enthusiasm for Mukhamedov's performance in *Giselle*. Aurelia is appalled. She never goes to the ballet, the audience just has no idea how to dress.

The Seasonal Shop Assistant

Harriet from Heathfield is the General Trading Company's Christmas ornament. After the exigencies of passing her A levels, the family holiday in Tuscany, her Leith's cookery course, the holiday with her friend Tara in St Tropez, her secretarial course and the holiday with her friend Oliver in Scotland, Harriet is being finished off in retail. It's awfully good fun working in the folderol department. Ollie is in toys at Harrods and Tara's bored silly in books so they all meet for drinks on the Fifth Floor of Harvey Nicks after work. These parameters will remain unchanged for the rest of Harriet's life; meanwhile she is saving for a back-packing trip round the Far East. Sensible, neat, with extremely clean hair, she is wonderfully polite and was a little hesitant with the customers at first. After all, they hadn't been formally introduced. Following Durham University she thinks she might like to work in public relations; a friend of Mummy's has a company that represents some brilliant shops so the GTC is terrific experience. If Harriet is not careful she could end up marrying a junior member of the Royal Family.

The Motorcycle Courier

The biker is the Romeo of the road. His black leathers, his gauntlets, his flowing (if slightly greasy) locks conspire to make him an object of desire for Lucinda, the photographer's assistant from Weybridge, who is now Juicy Lucy, Mike's bike chick, at weekends. They met when Greased Lightning Despatch sent Mike over to the studio to collect an urgent packet of contact sheets for *Vogue*. As Lucinda obeyed his masterful instructions – 'Sign here please, love' – she noted his blue eyes, raffish neckerchief and the insouciant way he held his Arai helmet under his arm like an extra head. Although, like others of his ilk, Mike carried on a guttural conversation with the static-distorted voice emitting from his shoulder, he always smiled at her and, several deliveries later, Lucy threw her leg across his trusty steed, a Kawasaki 500cc. Now her idea of Nirvana is Motorcycle City in Clapham and biking trips to the Isle of Wight with Mike's gang. Biking is so cool and one day Mike is going to get a Ducati. Or is it a Laverda? Anyway, it sounds really glamorous and Italian. Mike's dad, an accountant, can't understand why his son, after that expensive education at a minor public school, wants to hang around with bearded yobs in cafés. (And does he have proper insurance? One hears about the most dreadful accidents.) His mum thinks it's ever so nice that Mike works in the fresh air, but she worries about him living off fried eggs and Big Macs. What they don't know is that he's writing a film script. It's going to be mega. Stallone will definitely want to star as Mike.

The Winter Bridesmaid

Matilda is rweally, rweally cross. She's much too old to be a cissy bridesmaid, her petticoat is all scrwatchy and Nanny told her off in church for putting her fingers in her ears during 'Let the Bright Seraphim'. Having drunk, under cover of the speeches, the dregs of several glasses of champagne, Matilda has reached the argumentative stage of the inebriated. She doesn't want to dance with Daddy, and she certainly doesn't ever, ever want to see that stinky page-boy again. He pinched her, he did, Mummy, he did. It seemed such a good idea when her godmother asked Matilda to be a bridesmaid – a winter wedding, so romantic, and the velvet dress would be perfect for Christmas parties. 'Matilda is such a little tomboy, it will be so good for her – and, of course, she's *terribly* fond of you,' Matilda's mummy had added hastily. Matilda was bribed into a semblance of cordiality with hefty hints about the Present, if she behaved. Having imagined Power Rangers or roller blades, she was horribly sullen when, after the photographs, Godmother Venetia gave her a very small seed pearl necklace. Mummy says it will be lovely when she's grown up but Matilda doesn't want to be that sort of grown-up: seed pearls will look rweally silly with Caterpillar boots. Her fellow bridesmaids have been real goody-goodies and put their necklaces on straight away; Matilda righteously feels sick. Her elder cousin Rory, finding her dissecting her posy, suggests they use the roof of the marquee as a slide. Matilda is enchanted; since it has been raining all day, her dress will be ruined beyond all possibility of future parties. Weddings are grweat fun, Mummy, when can I be a brwidesmaid again?

The International Banker

The international banker would like to be a country squire but can never give up the income acquired by living at 35,000 feet between London, Hong Kong, Tokyo and New York. His children's names are a mystery to him and he has given up having an affair with his secretary since he married her as his second wife – a sad lack of imagination to which busy men are prone. His hooded, steely eyes (so effective at commanding clients' meetings) are actually the result of permanent jet-lag, and hairlines of executive stress have long since pulled his mouth into a thin slash, so the analyses of Sweden's desperate borrowing attempts emerge like the Delphic oracle through a letter-box. What is left of his hair (worrying about bonds, derivatives and collaring rates is so bald-making) is now smooth pepper and salt, like variegated patent leather. The impression, enhanced by his handmade suit from James & James, is of a suave streak of ruthlessness: finance ministers and corporate treasurers of more deeply indebted economies than ours are taken to the opera whether they like it or not. His house in the Peloponnese, his apartment in Aspen, his boat off the South of France are dim memories, the cumulative effect of years of cancelled holidays when the Pacific Rim seemed incapable of booming without him. The international banker lives in uncertain times; his son has failed to get into Eton, his wife has taken up the Harbour Club as a substitute lover and Augean clear-outs are all around him in the City. Or, if this is Thursday, is he on Wall Street?

The Chalet Girl

The ski chalet is Felicity's personal finishing school. At least, when she arrived in Val-d'Isère she was Felicity, but now she is Fluff, jolly perpetrator of spinach roulade and pork medallions in green peppercorn sauce. Fluff is a good girl with good teeth, good pearls and a good deal of weight since she acquired access to unlimited food and drink. It must be clearly understood that the punters are of secondary consideration to the Antipodean ski bum with whom she has nightly assignations in Dick's T-Bar. Also her skiing. Just because she's only nineteen and her most significant achievement at St Mary's was a GCSE in scripture, doesn't mean she can be pushed around by people from Surrey in C & A ski-wear. Daddy was a colonel, her mother an earl's second cousin twice removed and Felicity always scooped the school cup for hamster-keeping, enthusiasm and enterprise. The chalet girl has her standards: any punter making his/her own bed is rewarded with a Mars Bar on the pillow. Any punter who wishes to be preserved from the worst excesses of Fluff's two-week cookery course takes her Marmite, Golden Syrup and the latest copy of *Tatler*, and doesn't complain about the volatile hot water supply. No punter, having recoiled from a pine-clad cupboard advertised as a double bedroom, prefaces his first remarks to her with, 'It says in the brochure . . .' Come April, Fluff, panda-eyed and improbably blonde, will bounce home to Mummy in Chelsea. Once she's washed her leggings and caught up with her chums over capuccinos at the Dôme she'll be applying to prolong her suntan with a job in your villa in Corfu.

The Pantomime Dame

The pantomime dame is to theatre what Gaudi's architecture is to Barcelona – a gloriously vulgar extravagance covered with improbable knobbly bits. Upholstered in frills and ornamental frying pans he – or she as he is known – enters stage right ostensibly wreathed in dry ice. Actually it is cigar smoke. The dame's gruesome good humour is less to do with all the little perishers out there in the audience than having had a rattling good winner in the 3.30 at Haydock. Just the one in the Gargling Ferret has stoked the dame's inner certainty that his laundry scene is the best since the great days of Albert Modley; what the audience sees is that funny old codger who used to be on *Celebrity Squares* taking off thirteen pairs of bloomers to reveal underpants decorated with the Union Jack. In between the transformation scene ('You want a fairy coach? Whadda yer want him to teach?') and leading the song sheet with tyrannical Northern bonhomie ('Call that singing? I can't bloody hear you'), the dame calculates how long it will be before he can get away with the Wicked Stepmother – an ageing sit-com actress – to that swanky country house hotel in the Peak District.

The Bolshie Teenager

She has been to India in her gap year and, having returned to the throbbing sophistication of Gloucestershire and Chelsea, is now re-adjusting to materialism. Her father has manfully suppressed his horror about the stud in her nose ('It was wicked, this guy called Sanjay did it for me in Varanasi') and her mother now whips nervously through Royal tabloid stories at breakfast before confining their entrails to the log basket. Not that she need worry – the bolshie teenager doesn't wake for frivolty patrol until noon, by which time she expects her laundry, a *mélange* of trailing purply cotton, to have been processed by the daily. Her emaciation and spots first induced a maternal rush of fillet steak and M & S pawpaws but she just said, 'My body can't handle this rich food, Mum,' in the moment she could spare from peak-time telephone conversations with friends about her culture shock. God, isn't anyone in touch with *reality*? Everyone here just seems to think Harvey Nichols is Mother Teresa. Calcutta is seriously cool – God, the fragility of existence – and the wall hangings will look amazing in her study at Newcastle University.

The Interior Designer

Even the most uxorious of men would prefer their wives to have a lover than an interior designer. Like cancer, the first outbreak of interior designeritis may be small – a charmingly re-upholstered chair in the drawing room – and then, before you can say twenty thousand pounds, he has spread through the whole house. And all because nothing, my dear, went with the chair. The interior designer dismisses any footling objections to this excess with myriad examples of how much money he has actually saved: the marvellous rough calico thrown over a curtain pole in the dining room only cost £3·50 a metre from a man in Tooting. Naturally fifty metres were required in order to achieve the desired effect, but doesn't it look marvellous? It does. It took the interior designer's assistant, Carlos, an entire Saturday on double time to arrange it so artlessly and the gilded ram's head finial had to come from Paris. The susceptible – confidence in their own taste reduced to rubble – are shamelessly plied with fripperies: 'A Balinese wedding trunk is just what the hall needs.' Allegedly bought specially for them, it is actually the reject of a stronger-minded victim. Sanderson, china ornaments and Americans give the interior designer the vapours: 'I was literally asked to do everything for these people in Connecticut, they just moved in with their clothes. I even had to show them how to lay a table.' Just because the man wears cashmere doesn't mean he is not a bully.

The Rector's Wife

The rector's wife is exhausted by goodness. She has striven amongst the sick and the shiftless, brought and bought at every bring-and-buy necessitated by the perilous condition of the church roof and heroically suppressed her dislike of orange chrysanthemums. Mrs Armitage, with whom she does the altar flowers, thinks they add a lovely bit of colour. At Easter the Range Rover people in the Old Rectory (sold off by the Church Commissioners) give 'that poor little rector's wife' the run of their daffs as a gracious gesture to village life while they're away skiing. At home in the pebble-dash bungalow that now suffices as the nerve centre of four parishes, she makes a tasty supper out of leftovers, dutifully listens to her husband's sermon and thanks God for the thermal underwear which withstands the purist Anglican stance on heating. Her twin sister, who married a banker, looks half her age, having undergone total immersion in Donna Karan. Her kind M & S gift vouchers at Christmas induce a secret rage in the rector's wife that the Almighty is so unfair.

The Estate Agent

James the estate agent means well; it is not entirely his fault that he has landed up at Sloth and Greed. Daddy said that he'd cut off James's allowance unless he got a proper job (entrenched in Herefordshire, Daddy enjoys a misplaced optimism about 'the solid potential of bricks and mortar') and at least the toys are cool. James jumps into his Peugeot 205 and whizzes off to show Mrs Pernickety his one house of the day in Good Value Street (south of the river, but only ten minutes from Peter Jones). She is seething on the doorstep when he screams up, parking most of the Peugeot on the curb. 'Gosh, am I late? It's impossible parking round here – although they are bringing in a residents' scheme later in the year,' he adds hastily while fumbling with the wrong keys for the door. Once inside (the right keys having been retrieved from the deep litter of his glove compartment), James confidently leads the way saying, 'And this is the dining room,' while ushering Mrs Pernickety straight into the airing cupboard. She has a nose like a truffle hound for damp but her enquiries are obliterated by the shrill demands of James's mobile. His girlfriend/fellow estate agents want to know what time they are meeting for Mars Bar flavoured vodkas in Kartouche for, like a dinosaur's jawbone, James is a relic from the Jurassic era of the hard-drinking Sloane. As James tucks the telephone between his floppy haircut and his spotty cheeks and props his Filofax against the Laura Ashley wallpaper, Mrs Pernickety decides she is never, ever going to buy a house from a juvenile wearing an Hermès tie patterned with polar bears.

The Theatregoer

The theatregoer idolises Tom Stoppard without ever having understood a syllable of his work. Trips to the National Theatre are planned months in advance with her friend Beryl, an expert on the labyrinthine booking system, and they favour matinees, so much easier for the train home from Waterloo. Settling into the best of the cheapest stalls seats they meld with an audience of like-minded souls in comfy, neutral woollens which looks, *en masse*, like a vast sea of porridge. Indeed, the theatregoer is almost entirely handwoven, from her skirt and jumper, over which she toiled and spun, to her beads fashioned from painted seedpods. During the interval homemade sandwiches are produced from her Indian cotton patchwork handbag. Having lived so long and seen so much she has an encyclopaedic knowledge of the works of David Hare and the stamina to be bored senseless by three hours of anything Russian. The theatregoer is hardly the same sort of person who patronises *Copacabana* – that is not theatre, that is 'a show' – nor have she and Beryl given generously to Sir Andrew Lloyd Webber. *The Madness of George III* is about as frivolous as they are prepared to go and it has to be said that Alan Bennett fills them with unease because of his propensity to make jokes. A four-act drama about single parenting at the Tricycle theatre in Kilburn would be more reassuring since the theatregoer believes that anything turgid, difficult to get to by Tube or starring Vanessa Redgrave is intellectual.

The Master of Foxhounds

Major Comberledge bestrides his favourite hunter, Nellie, like a comfortable armchair. Comberledges of King's Comber have been masters of the Bedlington since his great-grandfather's day and neither a series of humdinging falls nor the rise of the anti-blood sports weasels (snivelling lefties, to a man) could ever persuade Hughie Comberledge that anything on God's earth beats a day's hunting. The blasted problem is the summer – too long, too hot and cluttered with holidays. He doesn't hold with abroad, had quite enough of it in the Blues and Royals and proper people should stay in their own homes. Give him a crisp winter's day, a good long point riding hard across the countryside and a kill at the end. Top of his list of dislikes are flashy newcomers in clean, new Isuzu Troopers (his own venerable Land Rover smells of saddle soap and wet dog) and flighty women on over-priced horses – they belong in one of those social, southern hunts that trot around people's back gardens. Nothing wrong with women, of course; he has several raw-boned former mistresses who hunt with him three times a week. Mrs Comberledge, too, had a splendid seat but has now taken up breeding Jacob sheep. The master's most steadfast relationship is with his kennels man, the gnarled and bow-legged Jim; together they plot the bloodlines of the hounds, all of whom Comberledge knows by name and finds more interesting than his own children. (His daughter, Serena, was a useful little rider until she discovered men and cigarettes.) A day concluded in a persuasive whisky with a tricky farmer is the most satisfactory: 'Now, Biggins, we don't want any hunt jumps on your land, y'know. Terrible tiger traps. Much safer to have big fences and kick on over.' And then home to a hot bath.

The Australian Nanny

The Australian nanny was brought up on thousands more acres than her employers. Life on a sheep station the size of Wales has made her resilient to weather, plumbing, illness and reptiles so the serpentine advances of Jack and Jemima's father are something with which she can easily deal, usually by a passion-crushing request for him to take the rubbish out. Unlike her English counterpart, who recoils from cleaning/shopping/dog-walking with a fastidious, 'Haven't you got someone else to do that?', Abbie the Aussie says, 'No worries,' and cooks to boot. She is invariably vegetarian because it's much safer when back-packing and the price of meat here is a sin to someone who has it running around at home. The children are transfixed by her stories of funnelweb spiders and the time she tipped a brown snake out of her little brother's cot, cornered it with a spade in the lounge and sawed its head off very carefully, so as not to mark her mum's new tiles. There is, sadly, not much opportunity for this sort of thing in Clapham. Abbie's employers are spellbound by the way she travels with an entire wardrobe seemingly contained in a pocket handkerchief, and cannot believe her capacity for alcohol on the Friday nights she spends with her mates who have also just arrived in London. She never has a hangover. Her weekends off are spent in Prague and she is carrying on a classified romance through the columns of *TNT* magazine, the Australian bible, with a Sydneysider she meet Inter-railing. Blissfully unaware of class distinction, Abbie is equally confident, polite and helpful with everyone she meets. When she leaves for California the entire family cries.

The Walker

The walker is the sophisticated woman's matching accessory. Lovers and husbands may come and go but the walker is a constant in the pantheon of first nights, opera galas and dinner parties. Well bred, well dressed, well heeled and well read, the walker is well aware of his importance in the scheme of things: without him a lot of women would be going nowhere. He loves women and is gratifyingly appreciative of the new dresses and hair that have required exhaustive decision-making, soothing away sartorial insecurity. 'Hermione, you were absolutely meant to be a blonde, it is God who got it wrong. Now guess who I saw having lunch at Le Caprice today?' With his exquisite taste in clothes, design and gossip, the walker is a far better companion than the brutish husbands with whom relationships have been clouded by sex and money. The walker's sexual preferences are diffuse. Suffice it to say that he is the antithesis of date rape; women may safely view the Auerbachs (which he collected while others were still struggling with the pronunciation) in his charming Chelsea apartment, noting also the Christmas cards from the Royal Family that he keeps on the mantelpiece all year round. The engraved invitations chart his social progress; he goes to Verona for Verdi, to New York to take Mrs Rich III to the Metropolitan Museum's soiree in the Temple of Dendara and to the South of France for the house parties, but darling, he always has time for *you*.

The Racegoer

(on front jacket)

Rowena Racegoer would look exactly the same upside down as she does the right way up, such is the accumulative effect of her colour co-ordination. That she is wearing an 'outfit', rather than real clothes, is why Rowena resembles one of those dolls designed to conceal the spare lavatory roll. She thinks the bizarre excrescence which is her hat looks *so* Philip Treacy and whispers to her friends that, if they swear not to tell another soul, she will give them the number of the marvellous little woman who ran it up in Bayswater. Rowena, who dabbles in public relations, is a fund of little women. She cannot bear to pay full price for anything when she can drive miles to uncharted parts of London to track the artisan to earth in a terraced house. Her suit was made specially for two weddings and Royal Ascot by 'someone who used to work for Hervé Leger'. Rowena is not married but umbilically attached to a source of funding called Roger, a property developer whose mouth is plugged with a large cigar. Not having a ticket to Number One car park, they eschew a picnic in favour of the reassuring expense of the seafood bar where they consume lobster and champagne, Rowena leaning outward, as if in a strong gale, to avoid dropping anything on her skirt. It is her secret ambition to be singled out for fashion comment on the television up there with Joan Collins and Ivana Trump, so she arrives early for the Royal procession and exchanges mwah-mwahs and darling-you-look-wonderfuls with other hats. Are there horses here? Only the weather-beaten countesses trotting between the paddock and the Tote. They are betting, Rowena is just out for a flutter.